General Richard S. Whitcomb loved Korea more than Koreans

한국인보다 한국을 더 사랑한

위트컴 장군

글·이근미 / 번역·문영한 / 그림·이진주
Author·Lee, Keun-mi / Translator·Moon, Young-han / Artist·Lee, Jin-ju

도서출판 물망초
Mulmangcho Books

차례 Contents

40계단과 불에 탄 축대 • 4
The forty steps and fire-burned terrace • 5

그 나라 국민을 위하는 것이 진정한 승리 • 18
The true victory is the one for the people of the country • 19

위트컴 장군의 한국 사랑, 부산 사랑 • 30
Gen Whitcomb's love for Korea and Busan • 31

한복 입고 모금에 나선 위트컴 장군 • 38
Gen Whitcomb dressed in Hanbok on the road for fundraising • 39

부산의 도시 기능을 살리다 • 44
The restoration of the city function of Busan • 45

부산대의 미래와 한국 청년의 도약을 위해 • 54
For the future of Pusan National University (PNU) as well as the Rise of the young generations in Korea • 55

한국유엔기념공원에 잠든 유일한 장성 • 60
The only general buried in the United Nations Memorial Cemetery in Korea (UNMCK) • 61

한국 고아의 아버지 • **70**
The father of Korean orphans • **71**

장진호에서 싸운 미 해병을 기억하라 • **80**
Remember the US Marines who fought in Chosin Reservoir (Jangjinho) • **81**

마미를 부르며 하늘나라로 간 미군들 • **86**
The US soldiers who went to Heaven calling ~ Mommies • **87**

국민훈장 무궁화장에 추서된 위트컴 장군 • **94**
Gen Whitcomb, posthumously honored by Mugunghwa Medal of Order, Civil Merit of Korea • **95**

한국인보다 더 한국을 사랑한 위트컴 장군 • **104**
Gen Whitcomb who loved Korea more than Korean people. • **105**

40계단과 불에 탄 축대

민아는 여름방학이 되어 아빠와 함께 부산 동광동 할머니댁에 왔어요.

적적하게 혼자 지내는 할머니와 함께 방학을 보낼 거예요.

부산 출장이 잦은 아빠가 종종 들르기로 한 데다 이웃에 고모도 살고 있어 걱정할 게 없어요.

할머니는 민아를 반갑게 맞아 주었어요. 할머니는 방학 동안 민아에게 맛있는 회국수도 만들어 주고 바다에도 데려가겠다고 약속했어요.

The forty steps and fire-burned terrace

Minah travelled to Busan with her Dad during summer vacation to visit her Grandma living in Dongkwangdong. Her Grandma lived so secluded and lonely by herself that Minah planned to spend a good time with Grandma. Fortunately, Minah's aunt lived nearby Grandma's house and Minah's father promised her to drop in Grandma's house as frequently as possible, using his available time on business trips to Busan. These made Minah relieved and happy. Grandma warmly welcomed Minah and promised her to cook yummy Sushi Noodles and take her to the beach.

저녁이 되어 좀 선선해지자 할머니와 민아가 손을 잡고 동네 산책을 나갔어요.

할머니는 집에서 가까운 40계단을 오르면서 말했어요.

"여기만 오면 옛날 생각이 나. 내가 어릴 때 부모님 손잡고 오르내린 계단이니까. 피란민들이 계단에 앉아 영도다리를 바라보며 향수를 달랬지."

할머니와 보조를 맞춰 천천히 40계단을 올라 맨 위에서 조금 쉬다가 다시 내려오는 게 순서예요. 오늘은 할머니가 민아의 손을 잡고 계단 위 도로를 건너 골목으로 들어갔어요. 조금 걷다가 어느 집 축대 앞에 서더니 할머니가 돌을 쓰다듬었어요.

"내가 이 동네에서 오래 살면서도 이 시커먼 축대가 불에 그을린 흔적이라는 걸 몰랐어. 너희 고모가 신문에 불탄 축대에 대한 기사가 났다며 읽어줘서 이번에 알았지. 내가 아주 어릴 때 이 동네에 큰불이 난 적 있거든."

민아는 할머니가 가리키는 축대를 만져보았어요.

거뭇거뭇한 돌이 낮 동안 달구어져서 아직 따뜻했어요.

"그 기사에 그동안 잊고 있었던 위트컴 장군님 이름도 나오고 동상을 세운다는 소식도 있어서 얼마나 놀라고 감사했던지."

민아는 처음 들어보는 위트컴 장군이 누군지 궁금했어요.

"위트컴 장군님이 누구야? 할머니랑 알아?"

"알다마다. 민아가 지금 열 살이지? 내가 그 나이에 위트컴 장군님을 만났잖아."

"와, 신기하다. 위트컴 장군님을 어디서 만났어?"

As it became cooler in the evening, Minah and Grandma took a walk holding hands. Grandma began to speak as they climbed up the Forty Steps.

"This spot reminds me of the old times, because when I was young, I normally used to walk up and down these stairs with my parents. I remember that war refugees, sitting on these stone-made stairs and staring at the Youngdo Bridge, soothed their homesickness."

It was a routine for Minah and Grandma to take slow walks up and down the stairs with a short break at the top. But today, Grandma held Minah's hand and led her to the small alleyway across the road at the top of the stairs. When they walked a few more steps, Grandma suddenly stopped in front of the terrace of a certain house, and softly began to touch the stones of the terrace.

"I have not recognized this black terrace was the scar of the fire-burned evidence even though I had lived a long time on this street. I recently learned the facts about the fire-burned terrace through your aunt. Hearing from her newspaper reading, I knew there had been a big fire in the past in this street. "

Minah touched the terrace which Grandma pointed at. The darkish and tanned stone has been heated during the daytime and kept warm.

"I was very frightened and grateful from the news to hear the name of General Whitcomb whom I forgot for a while, and the plan to erect his statue.

"Gen Whitcomb? Who was he? Did you know him? "

"Of course I know. Hmm, You are ten years old now, Minah? I met him when I was at your age."

"Wow, amazing! Where did you meet him?"

민아의 재촉에 할머니는 빙그레 웃으며 말했어요.

"집에 가서 이야기해줄게. 옛날 생각하면 힘든 일이 떠올라 일부러 잊으려고 노력했는데 위트컴 장군님 이름을 들으니 다 생각나네."

집으로 돌아와 저녁을 먹고 나자 할머니가 "내 이름은 김순이야. 열 살 때 순이 얘기 들어볼래?"라고 했어요. 민아는 잔뜩 기대하고 할머니를 바라봤어요.

내가 열 살 때 부산에 왔단다. 부모님 손에 이끌려 북한 흥남부두에서 미군 배를 타고 와 이리저리 떠돌다 영주동 산동네에 자리 잡았지. 판자로 얼기설기 엮은 집은 겨우 바람만 막는 정도였어. 지붕은 미군부대에서 나온 기름종이로 덮었어. 다들 비가 새지 않는 기름종이를 구하려고 애썼지. 방 하나와 부엌이 전부였지만 부모님은 이런 집이라도 있어서 정말 다행이라고 하셨어.

Grandma lightly smiled and responded to Minah's urge.

"O.K, I will tell you the whole story when we are back home. I try not to think about this miserable accident because it reminds me of my hard times in the old days. But after hearing the name of Gen Whitcomb, the whole situation of that time comes to me again."

They went back home and had supper, soon after, Grandma started to speak.

"Minah, my name is Kim, Sooni. Are you interested in 'The tale of Ten Year Old Girl, Sooni'?" Minah looked up at her Grandma with eager anticipation.

I came to Busan at the age of ten. My family was evacuated from North Korea (NK) during the Korean War (6.25 war). We escaped from Hungnam Port by the help of the US navy ship. Thereafter, we arrived in Busan, wandered here and there, and finally settled down in the mountainous area of Youngjudong. We lived in a small shelter which was temporarily built by a few pieces of the wooden boards, and could be just protected from the winds. The roof was covered by the oil-coated papers, and most of them were outflows from US military camps. At that time, the refugees struggled to get some oil-coated papers since the material was very strong against rain. Though our house was just a tiny one, having only a room and a small kitchen, my parents used to say that we were lucky to even have a house like this.

북한 공산당이 쳐들어와서 부산지역만 겨우 남았을 때였어. 부산지역은 유일하게 6·25 때 전쟁을 겪지 않아 전국에서 피란민이 몰려들었고, 산꼭대기까지 판잣집이 들어섰지. 허술한 집들이 다닥다닥 붙어있어서인지 불이 자주 났어. 그래서 부산을 불산이라고 부를 정도였어.

　날씨가 점점 추워지면서 집집마다 나무를 주워다 불을 땠어. 엄마는 불이 나면 크게 번진다며 걱정을 많이 했어. 1953년 11월 27일이었어. "불이야! 불이야!"하는 소리에 아버지가 빨리 나가자며 내 손을 잡았어. 엄마는 그 와중에도 보따리에다 닥치는 대로 물건들을 쌌어. 아버지가 빨리 가자고 채근했고, 우리 세 식구가 마구 달려 내려왔지. 오다가 보니까 불붙은 기름종이가 둥둥 떠다니면서 여기저기 불을 옮기고 있었어. 기름종이 쪼가리가 엄마 다리에 달라붙어서 아버지가 급하게 껐어. 얼마나 데었는지 살펴볼 겨를도 없이 다시 달렸지. 울퉁불퉁한 언덕에서 내가 제대로 못 달리니까 아버지가 나를 업고 아랫동네까지 왔어.

The NK Communist Forces abruptly invaded South Korea, and Busan was the only area left unconquered. As Busan was uniquely spared by the war, the refugees rushed there, and the area was filled with wooden-board houses which occupied all of the mountainous area. These fragile houses densely stood shoulder by shoulder, therefore causing frequent fires, producing the notorious nickname, Bulsan (which means fire-city Busan).

As the weather became colder, most of the refugees used woods for heating. My mother was very concerned it might cause a big fire that would spread. On 27th Nov, 1953, we heard big shouting, 'Fire~ Fire~' in the street, and my Dad grabbed my hand and rushed outside. Mom tried to pack up a few things in spite of the risky situation. As my father urged prompt action, my family rapidly ran down the street. During our escape, we saw fire-burning oil papers flying around the air and spreading the fire here and there. One of the fire-burning oil papers got stuck to my Mom's leg, but Dad quickly put it out. There was no time to examine how seriously Mom was burned, and we kept running and running. Since I was very weak in running up the rugged hill, Dad carried me on his back and ran down to town.

영주동 산비탈 판자촌에서 시작된 불이 동광동과 부산역까지 번져 모두 잿더미가 됐어. 아까 봤던 돌로 쌓은 축대 정도만 남은 거지. 그 화재로 6,000여 가구가 피해를 입고 29명의 사상자가 발생했대. 3만여 명이나 되는 사람들이 오갈 데가 없어진 거야.

"큰일이네. 겨울을 어디서 지낸대요."
"1월에도 국제시장에 불이 나서 다 타버렸는데, 어휴 뭐가 남아나질 않네."
　그런 대화를 나누는 부모님의 얼굴이 어두웠어. 어른들은 정부에 돈이 없어 우리를 도울 수 없을 거라며 걱정했어. 전쟁이 3년간 계속되다가 그해 7월 27일에서야 휴전했거든.
　메리놀수녀의원에 화상입은 사람이 2,000명이나 몰려갔대. 6·25 전쟁이 나기 직전인 1950년 4월에 수녀님들이 가난한 사람들을 무료로 치료해주기 위해 세운 곳이야. 아버지가 빨리 껐는데도 엄마 오른쪽 다리에 수포가 생기고 진물이 흘렀어. 외국인 수녀님이 엄마를 잘 치료해주어서 나았지. 한동안 고생하긴 했지만.

The fire which originated from the wooden-board houses in Youngjudong gradually spread to Donggwangdong, to the Busan railroad station, and finally turned the whole area into a big ash dregs. The stone-made terrace as you just saw was the only structure that survived. The fire was at last extinguished, but 6,000 families were impacted. There were 29 deaths and injuries, and about 30,000 people were displaced.

My parents said to each other, "This is a terrible disaster! Where and how can we survive this winter?"

"A big fire also occurred in Busan's International Market last January. Nothing could be saved from there."

Their faces darkened. Grown ups worried and said that the Government had no funds left to help us as the 3-year-long 6.25 war had just ended with the signing of the Armistice Treaty last 27th July.

Almost 2,000 injured people rushed to the Maryknoll Sister's Clinic. The Clinic was founded in 1950 just before the 6.25, primarily to provide medical services to poor people in Korea. Though my Dad barely put out the burning on mother's leg, the spot already made the water-blister leaking white and yellow liquid out of the sores. But the kind nuns treated her wounds well and she made full recovery although it was painful for a while.

그 나라 국민을 위하는 것이 진정한 승리

　민아는 열 살밖에 안 된 순이가 고생한 걸 생각을 하니 눈물이 났어요. 민아는 서울의 좋은 아파트에서 너무도 편하게 지낸다는 걸 새삼 깨닫고 부모님께 감사한 마음이 들었어요. 다음 이야기가 궁금해서 할머니를 졸랐어요.
　"할머니, 순이 어떻게 해. 집이 다 타버렸잖아. 걱정이야."
　"에휴, 그때 생각하니 가슴이 갑갑하네. 참 힘든 시절이었지."
　할머니가 한숨을 후 내쉬고 말을 이어갔어요.

The true victory is the one for the people of the country

Minah felt tears rolling down her cheeks thinking about the difficulties the ten-year old girl Sooni was going through. As she thought about her happy life living in a comfortable home in Seoul, she was very grateful for her parents. She was curious about the next story and urged Grandma to continue.

"Grandma, your house was burned to the ground. Poor Sooni. What is she going to do?"

"Ah~, it was a very difficult time."

Grandma sighed and continued.

집이 다 타버려 갈 데가 없으니 밖에서 며칠간 떨며 지냈지. 우리뿐만 아니라 그런 사람이 많았어. 어느 날 키 크고 코가 뾰족한 미군들이 왔어. 어깨에 별 하나를 단 미군이 영어로 말을 하니까 한국 군인이 통역해줬어.

"여러분, 나는 유엔군 부산 군수기지 사령관 리차드 위트컴입니다. 곧 대형 텐트를 쳐서 여러분이 따뜻하게 지내도록 하겠습니다. 식량도 지원해서 굶지 않게 돕겠습니다."

제대로 먹지도 못한 채 오돌오돌 떨고 있던 사람들이 그 말을 듣고 이제 살았다며 안도했어.

바로 미군 공병부대원들이 와서 바닥을 평평하게 고르고 대형 텐트를 치기 시작했어. 큰 텐트 하나에 몇 집씩 들어가서 살게 되었어. 미군들이 침대와 이불까지 다 마련해주고 옷과 식량도 나눠줬어. 텐트 안에서 따뜻하게 지내며 위트컴 장군님과 미군들에게 감사했지.

얼마 지나지 않아 미군들이 텐트 안에 나무를 세웠어. 거기에 솜도 얹고 솔방울도 달았어. 나는 그게 크리스마스 트리라는 걸 처음 알았어. 크리스마스 날 위트컴 장군님이 텐트마다 방문해서 아이들에게 선물을 나누어 주었어. 나는 분홍색 표지의 예쁜 노트를 선물로 받았어. 그런 고급 노트를 처음 받아 정말 기뻤어. 그때부터 분홍색을 좋아하게 됐지.

The house was completely destroyed and my family and I had to spend the next few days outside in the cold. There were also many others who were placed in difficult circumstances. One day, some tall men in US military uniforms with pointed noses approached us. There, an army general with one-star badge on his shoulder said something in English which a Korean soldier interpreted.

"Hello, everybody, my name is Richard Whitcomb, Commander of the 2nd Logistics Command of the United Nations Command (UNC). We will set up large tents soon to keep you warm and also will provide you with food."

People were relieved to hear the general's speech after days of worrying, shivering and feeling hungry. Soon after, the engineering troops came, levelled the ground and began to set up tents. The tents were big enough to accomodate a few households in one. The Americans also provided beds and blankets as well as clothes and food. We thanked Gen Whitcomb and his soldiers for the comfortable tents and supplies. Some time later, American soldiers came again and put up a wooden pole inside the tent, and decorated it with cotton balls and pine cones. I learned that it was a Christmas tree. On Christmas Day, Gen Whitcomb visited every tent and gave children Christmas gifts. A pretty pink notebook was given to me, and it was the most fantastic gift I ever had in my life. Since that day, pink has been my favorite color.

우리는 철모르고 뛰어놀았지만 어른들은 모이기만 하면 걱정했어. 겨울은 텐트에서 난다 해도 봄이 오면 어떻게든 다시 집을 지어야 한다며 한숨을 쉬었어.

우리가 사는 텐트에 일곱 집이 살았는데 박씨 아저씨네도 있었어. 미군부대에 다니는 박씨 아저씨가 소식통이어서 어른들이 우리 텐트에 자주 모였어. 어느 날 저녁, 박씨 아저씨가 급하게 들어오더니 걱정스러운 목소리로 말했어.

"위트컴 장군님이 미국으로 소환되었대. 감옥에 갈 수도 있대. 이 텐트하고 침대, 이불, 식량 같은 게 전부 군수물자라는 거야. 군인들을 위한 물자를 민간인한테 준 게 큰 죄라고 하네."

박씨 아저씨의 말에 어른들은 우리 때문에 장군님이 벌 받으면 어떡하느냐고 걱정했어.

At that time, we were just young kids who were clueless about what was going on in the real world, but the grown ups sighed and worried about having to build new houses when spring comes, even if they could survive this winter in the tents.

Seven families lived together in our tent, and Mr. Park's family was one of them. Mr. Park was working at the US military camp, so he always had the latest news of the US military situation, and people used to get together in our tent. One evening, Mr. Park hastily entered the tent and said gravely,

"I heard the news that Gen Whitcomb was summoned to his country. He could go to jail for his misconduct of giving us beds, blankets, foods, etc, which were meant to be military supplies. It is said to be unlawful in the US to use military supplies for civilian use."

The people were frightened to hear Mr. Park's comments and worried that Gen Whitcomb would get in trouble for helping us.

얼마 후, 박씨 아저씨가 위트컴 장군님이 미국에서 돌아오셨다는 소식을 알려주었어.

"위트컴 장군님이 미국으로 소환되었을 때 군법회의에 회부된 데다 미국 의회 청문회까지 불려 갔대. 의원들이 위트컴 장군님한테 '왜 군수물자를 군인이 아닌 민간인들에게 나눠줬습니까. 군인들이 쓸 물건이 없으면 어떡합니까?' 하고 막 소리 질렀다는 거야."

박씨 아저씨의 얘기에 다들 잔뜩 긴장한 표정을 지었어.

"그때 위트컴 장군님이 큰소리로 '전쟁은 총칼로만 하는 게 아닙니다. 그 나라 국민을 위하는 것이 진정한 승리입니다' 하고 외치자 시끄럽던 의회장이 일순간에 조용해졌대. 한 의원이 박수를 치니까 여기저기서 일어나서 박수를 쳤다는군."

박씨 아저씨의 말에 텐트 안에 있던 어른들도 박수를 쳤어.

"그때 어떤 의원이 '여러분 전쟁이 막 끝난 시점이라 한국 사정이 매우 어렵습니다. 위트컴 장군에게 구호금을 모아주어 한국이 일어설 수 있도록 도웁시다'라고 했대. 그러자 의원들이 '옳소, 옳소'하며 박수를 쳤다는 거야. 구호금 모아주자고 한 의원님도 참 고마운 분이야."

박씨 아저씨의 말에 또다시 박수가 쏟아졌어.

Some time later, Mr. Park brought the latest good news that Gen Whitcomb had returned to Korea.

"When Gen Whitcomb was summoned to America, he was court martialed and subpoenaed to Congress Hearing. The congressmen rudely asked Gen Whitcomb, 'Why did you give military supplies to civilians? Didn't you think about our soldiers' needs?' "

The people in the tent went quiet upon hearing this. Mr. Park continued,

"At that very moment, Gen Whitcomb stood up and spoke in loud voice, 'War is done with weapons and it remains undone, unless it is done for the people in the country'. Shortly after his remarks, the conference hall fell silent. One congressman began to clap, and many fellow congressmen followed with applause."

People in the tent started clapping too upon hearing this.

Mr. Park continued, "A congressman then suggested, 'Fellow members, the situation in post-Korea is dire. How about we raise money for Gen Whitcomb to help Korea's recovery?' Most of congressmen clapped and shouted 'yes!~ yes!~' We should be grateful for the congressman who proposed relief money for Korea."

People in the tent began clapping at Mr. Park's good news.

그로부터 며칠 후 위트컴 장군님이 놀라운 선물을 갖고 왔어.

"여러분, 미국에서 받아온 원조금으로 여러분이 앞으로 살 주택을 짓기로 했습니다."

모이기만 하면 집 걱정을 했던 어른들이 놀라서 입을 다물지 못했어. 우리 엄마는 눈물까지 흘렸어. 아직 겨울이 채 가지도 않았는데 온통 따뜻한 기운이 넘치는 것 같았어.

A few days later, Gen Whitcomb came by with a surprise. He said, "Fellow citizens, we have relief funds provided by the US government, and I plan to use the money to build houses for you." Grown ups, who were always worried about a place to live, could not believe this news. My mother sobbed. Though it was still the middle of winter, we felt warmth all around us.

위트컴 장군의 한국 사랑, 부산 사랑

민아는 마치 텐트 안에서 박씨 아저씨 얘기를 직접 들은 것처럼 마음이 따뜻해졌어요. 순이네 집이 생긴다니 정말 다행이라는 생각이 들었어요. 어린 순이와 부모님, 그리고 동네 사람들을 도와준 위트컴 장군님이 무척 고마웠어요. 정말 집을 지었는지, 언제까지 텐트에 있었는지 모든 게 궁금했어요. 할머니의 이야기가 계속됐어요.

어느덧 한 해가 가고 나는 열한 살이 되었어. 배가 점점 불러오던 영식이 엄마가 곧 아기를 낳을 거라고 했어. 며칠 후 영식이 엄마가 산통이 시작되어 막 소리를 지르자 영식이 아빠와 우리 엄마가 영식이 엄마를 부축해서 텐트 옆에 있는 보리밭으로 갔어.

나는 영식이하고 텐트 앞에서 조마조마한 마음으로 기다리고 있었어. 멀리서 아기 울음소리가 들렸을 때 나도 모르게 영식이 손을 잡고 폴짝폴짝 뛰었어. 그때 위트컴 장군님이 텐트촌에 왔어. 아기 목청이 어찌나 큰지 울음소리가 계속 들렸어.
"어디서 아기 울음 소리가 나는 거야?"
위트컴 장군님이 통역을 통해 물었어.
"저기서 영식이 엄마가 아기를 낳았어요. 텐트에 여러 집이 사니까 아기 낳기가 곤란해 보리밭으로 간 거예요."
내 설명을 들은 위트컴 장군님이 고개를 끄덕이며 근심스런 표정을 지었어.

Gen Whitcomb's love for Korea and Busan

Minah was deeply moved by the story and felt as though she were in the tent listening to Mr. Park. She was excited to hear that Sooni's family was soon going to have a house to live in. She was very grateful for Gen Whitcomb's helping Sooni's family and the neighbours. But she was anxious to know whether the houses were really built, and how long they had stayed in the tent. Grandma's story continued.

A year had passed and I turned eleven. Youngshik's mother was heavily pregnant and the baby was due soon. One day, Youngshik's mother started labor and began moaning. Youngsik's father and my mother took her to a barley field nearby.

I was waiting with Youngshik in front of the tent nervously. Then there was a baby's cry, which made me grab Youngshik's hand and jump up and down with excitement. At that moment, Gen Whitcomb came by our tent, and asked where the baby's big cry was coming from through his translator. "There, barley field! Youngshik's mother just gave birth. The tent was not a proper place for childbirth because it was shared by many people. That's why she went to the barley field to give birth." Gen Whitcomb nodded with a concerned look on his face.

영식이 엄마가 텐트에서 예쁜 아기를 안고 누워있을 때 위트컴 장군님이 다시 방문했어.

"영도구 피란민촌에 아기를 낳을 수 있는 산원을 마련할 겁니다. 앞으로 거기서 아기를 낳으면 됩니다."

세심한 부분까지 신경 쓰는 위트컴 장군님이 참 고마웠어. 그날 위트컴 장군님이 메리놀병원을 아주 크게 지을 거라고 말했어.

"미국에 불려갔다가 돌아올 때 받아온 구호금으로 AFAK라는 단체를 만들었어요. '미군대한원조처'라는 뜻입니다. 이 단체에서 많은 일을 할 텐데 메리놀수녀의원을 지상 3층 160병상 규모의 종합병원으로 확대할 계획입니다."

Gen Whitcomb visited our tent again. Youngshik's mother was holding her cute baby. He announced, "We will build a maternity ward at the refugee camp in Youngdogu, so women can give birth there in the future." I was happy to hear the news and extremely grateful that Gen Whitcomb was thinking about every aspect of our lives. Later that day, he announced the plan to build Maryknoll Hospital.

"While I was back in the US, we received a grant which enabled us to establish AFAK (Armed Forces Aid to Korea). This organization will do much good for Korea, including a plan expand the Maryknoll Sister's clinic to a general hospital, which will have three floors and 160 beds."

그 말을 들은 엄마가 몹시 기뻐했어. 수녀님들이 좋은 환경에서 일하게 된 데다 더 많은 환자가 치료받게 되었으니까.

곧 메리놀병원 공사가 시작됐지만 생각만큼 빨리 진척되지 않았어. 박씨 아저씨가 그 이유를 설명해줬어.

"돈이 부족해서 그렇지. AFAK에서 여러 가지 사업을 하니까. 지금 우리 이재민들 집도 짓고 있잖아. 그래서 위트컴 장군님이 미군 장병들에게 기부를 부탁하셨대. 월급의 1%를 메리놀병원 짓는 데 기부해달라고. 고맙게도 미군들이 기꺼이 동참하겠다고 했대."

어른들이 이구동성으로 참 고마운 군인들이라고 말했어.

"미국 속담에 '밥은 굶어도 기부는 한다'는 말이 있대. 미국 사람들은 어릴 때부터 기부하는 게 습관이 되어 있다잖아. 기독교 국가여서 성경의 가르침대로 이웃 돕는 걸 당연하게 여긴대."

박씨 아저씨 말에 어른들이 "그런 습관은 우리도 본받아야 돼"라고 말했어.

My mom was very glad to hear that news, for the nuns to work in better conditions and more patients to receive care.

Soon, the construction of Maryknoll Hospital began, but the progress was slow. Mr. Park explained the reason why. "Lack of money is the main reason. AFAK has been pursuing several projects including the current construction of new houses. So, Gen Whitcomb asked for US soldiers to donate. One percent of salary for donation was suggested for the building of Maryknoll Hospital, and thankfully, the soldiers willingly joined in."

The grown ups in the tent praised the soldiers for being such good friends. Mr. Park continued, "I heard that there is a saying in US, 'Even though I am starving, I would donate'. Americans have a tradition of giving. America is a Christian country and the Bible teaches them to look after their neighbors in need."

People nodded and said, "We Koreans should do the same."

한복 입고 모금에 나선 위트컴 장군

민아는 할머니 이야기를 들을수록 감동이 차올랐어요. 가난한 우리나라에 도움을 준 손길을 절대 잊으면 안 된다는 생각이 들었어요. 할머니 얘기를 듣다 보니 갑자기 궁금한 게 있었어요.

"할머니, 영식이는 어떻게 됐어? 영식이 동생은?"

"이제 할아버지 할머니가 됐겠지. 여러 곳에 지은 이재민 주택으로 흩어진 뒤로 못 만났어. 요즘같이 핸드폰을 쓸 때가 아니니까."

할머니 얼굴이 좀 서운해 보였어요. 할머니가 계속 이야기를 이어갔어요.

Gen Whitcomb dressed in Hanbok on the road for fundraising

Minah was deeply moved by Grandma's story, and she resolved never to forget the help which Korea received in those difficult times. And suddenly she thought about the baby.

"Grandma, what became of Youngshik and his baby sister?"

"They would be old by now. I have had no connection with them since we left the tents and went to different refugee settlements. It was not like now. We didn't have mobile phones then."

Grandma looked little bit sad, and went on talking.

어느 날 눈이 휘둥그레지는 장면을 봤어. 키가 크고 덩치가 큰 위트컴 장군님이 한복에다 갓까지 쓰고 있었거든. 늘 군복 차림이던 위트컴 장군님이 한복을 입고 있으니 이상했어. 왜 그런 모습으로 거리를 누비는지 아줌마들의 대화로 곧 알게 됐어.

"장군이라는 사람이 체신머리 없이 왜 저래."

"그런 말 마. 눈길을 끌어 모금을 많이 하려고 그러는 거지."

"얼마나 고마운 분인데. 늘 우리를 도와주시는 분이야."

One day, I was shocked to see Gen Whitcomb, who was very tall, dressed in Hanbok, completed with Gat (Korean traditional hat) on his head. It was odd to see him in Hanbok, since I was used to seeing him in his military uniform. But I soon found out why he was walking around in Hanbok from the village women who were gossiping.

"What made him behave like that? Isn't he a general?"

"Hey, don't talk about him like that. He is trying to get people's attention for fundraising."

"We should be thankful. He is always trying to help us."

어른들의 말을 들으며 위트컴 장군님이 정말 고마운 분이라고 생각했어. 아무리 기부를 잘하는 미국인이라지만 위트컴 장군님의 한국 사랑, 부산 사랑은 정말 대단했어.

저녁에 어른들도 한복입고 모금하러 다닌 위트컴 장군님 얘기로 꽃을 피웠어. 박씨 아저씨가 더 놀랄 일이 있다고 했어.

"전쟁 끝난 지 얼마 안 되어 정부에 돈이 없잖아. 그래서 부산의 각 기관들이 다 어렵대. 돈이 없어서 복구 사업을 하려고 해도 엄두를 낼 수 없다는 거야. 그걸 아신 위트컴 장군님이 88개 미군부대를 부산지역의 각 기관과 다 연결해주셨대. 예하 부대원들에게 자원봉사도 하고 안 입는 옷, 안 쓰는 물건도 많이 기부해달라는 당부까지 하셨대."

박씨 아저씨 말에 감동해서 눈물을 닦는 어른도 있었어.

"공사할 일이 있으면 미군들이 나서서 직접 해주라는 부탁까지 하셨대. 여기 텐트촌 지을 때도 미군들이 와서 바닥 고르고 바로 완성했잖아. 미군들은 기술도 좋고 장비도 많아 빨리빨리 잘하니까."

박씨 아저씨가 "위트컴 장군님이 한국에 부임하신 건 하나님의 선물이야"라고 덧붙이자 다들 "맞아, 맞아"라며 맞장구를 쳤어.

위트컴 장군님이 도와준 덕분에 텐트에 살던 사람들은 이재민 주택에 입주했고, 메리놀병원도 완공됐지. 우리도 예쁘고 따뜻한 집을 갖게 되었어.

Their conversation filled me with so much gratitude to Gen Whitcomb. He seemed to be such a generous person, and his love for Korea and Busan was amazing.

In the evening, the story of Gen Whitcomb's fundraising dressed in Hanbok was all the grown ups talked about. Mr. Park surprised everyone by saying,

"Our government has run out of money because of the war. No government agencies in Busan have budget for any restoration projects. Gen Whitcomb recognized the situation and he let the 88 US military units be connected with the agencies of Busan. Moreover, he requested that soldiers volunteer their time and donate clothes and other supplies."

Some of the grown ups quietly wiped their eyes.

"The General even requested that soldiers help out with construction if needed. Remember how efficiently they levelled the ground and built the tents? American soldiers are skillful and have good equipments."

When Mr. Park added, "It was truly God's blessing that Gen Whitcomb was sent to Korea", everybody joined in and said "Yes! Yes! Absolutely!".

Thanks to Gen Whitcomb, the refugees were able to leave the tents and move into the newly built houses. My family also moved into a nice and cozy house.

부산의 도시 기능을 살리다

할머니 얘기가 끝났을 때 민아는 먼 옛날로 여행을 다녀온 것 같은 기분이었어요.
"이렇게 훌륭한 위트컴 장군님의 동상을 세운다는데 모금이 안 될까 봐 걱정이다. 한 사람이 만 원씩 3만 명이 내야 한다는데, 그게 될지 모르겠네."

1953년 큰불이 났을 때 위트컴 장군님이 3만 명의 이재민을 도운 은혜에 보답하기 위해 부산 시민 3만 명이 1인당 만 원씩 내서 동상을 세우기로 했다는 거예요. 1년 동안 3억 원을 모으는 게 목표라고 했어요.

"오래전 일인 데다 그때 영주동하고 동광동, 부산역 쪽에 사는 사람들만 도움받았는데 다른 동네 사람들이 돈을 낼까? 돈이 안 모아지면 어쩌지?"
할머니의 한숨에 민아는 엄마가 방학 때 쓰라고 준 용돈에서 만 원을 꺼냈어요.

The restoration of the city function of Busan

When Grandma finished her long story, Minah felt she seemed to have travelled backward long time ago.

"I was little bit concerned that the fundraising for the erection of the statue of Gen Whitcomb, such a admirable character, would not go well. Would the plan of raising 10,000 won per person be successful?"

The idea of raising 10,000 won per person originated from the remembrance of big fire in Busan occurred in 1953. At that time, Gen Whitcomb helped 30,000 disaster victims, and people decided to erect the statue of him to cherish his distinguished service. Therefore, donation of 10,000 won per person for 30,000 citizens of Busan was proposed. The goal was to raise 300 million won within a year.

"Since it was remembered an old story and most of the beneficiaries were localized in Youngjudong/ Donggwangdong area, and the vicinity of Busan station, I doubt whether the people of other areas would join in this donation project. I am nervous about the slow fundraising."

As Grandma sighed, Minah took 10,000 won from her purse which was a bit of portion her mother gave her for summer vacation.

"할머니, 나도 성금낼게. 할머니 얘기 들으니까 위트컴 장군님은 정말 훌륭한 분이야. 꼭 동상을 세워야 돼."

할머니는 민아의 머리를 쓰다듬으며 기특하다고 칭찬했어요.

마침 이웃에 사는 고모가 왔어요.

민아는 고모에게 위트컴 장군님을 아는지 물었어요.

"요즘 엄마가 위트컴 위트컴 노래를 해서 검색 해봤더니 부산을 위해 정말 많은 일을 하셨더라."

고모는 AFAK를 통해 5년 동안 600만 달러나 지원했다는 걸 알고 놀랐다고 했어요.

"그 돈으로 이재민을 돕고 부산의 도시 기능을 살리기 위해 많은 일을 했더라. 우리 돈으로 환산하면 70억 원 정도 되는데 70년 전에 70억 원은 어마어마한 액수야. 그 가운데 절반을 부산 역전 대화재 복구에 썼대."

고모도 감동을 많이 받은 표정이었어요.

"Grandma, I would also like to participate in fundraising. I fully recognized that Gen Whitcomb is very respectable man, and I dare say that his statue should be erected."

Grandma touched Minah's head and applauded for her praiseworthy behavior.

Just then, Minah's Aunt living neighbour to Grandma dropped, and Minah asked her whether she recognized Gen Whitcomb.

"Recently, my mom repeatedly sings a song of Gen Whitcomb, so I searched his name and I found out he really had done lots of good things for Busan."

Aunt said she was so surprised to know Gen Whitcomb had supported 6 US million dollars for Busan in five years through AFAK.

"With that money, the General did lots of things to help the disaster victims and to restore the city functions of Busan. 6 US million dollars would be calculated by approximately 7 billion Korean Won at 70 years ago which seemed to be an enormous amount of money. The half of that money was spent for the restoration of the Busan station which was devastated by fire."

Aunt looked also deeply impressed, and continued,

"될성부른 나무는 떡잎부터 안다더니 위트컴 장군님은 어릴 때부터 달랐더라. 부모님을 따라 교회에 열심히 다니고, 아버지는 법대 교수, 엄마는 작가로 풍족한 집안인데도 목장에서 아르바이트를 했대. 휴일이면 누가 시키지 않아도 대걸레와 물통을 들고 2층부터 아래층까지 청소했다더라. 민아도 방학동안 청소 열심히 할 거지?"

고모의 말의 말에 민아가 고개를 끄덕였어요.

"위트컴 장군님은 어떻게 그렇게 똑똑하고 헌신적이었을까. 세상에나, 참 훌륭한 분이야."

할머니의 말에 고모가 "한마디로 풍부한 경험 덕이지"라고 했어요.

"위트컴 장군님은 제1차 세계대전에 참전한 이후 기업과 정부 기관에 근무하면서 업무 경험을 많이 쌓았더라구. 주지사 후보로 거론될 만큼 촉망받았는데 1941년 미국이 제2차 세계대전 참전을 결정하자 대령으로 입대해 아이슬란드와 영국, 프랑스를 돌며 지휘관으로 근무했대."

"우리나라에 오기 전에도 전쟁에 많이 참여했구나. 세상에나."

할머니의 말에 고모가 고개를 끄덕였어요.

"As we know the old saying 'A mature tree begins with its cotyledons', Gen Whitcomb was an example of this phrase. He was quite distinguished from other boys in his young ages. He faithfully participated in church services with his parent, worked part-time jobs in the ranch in spite of being a son of wealthy family. His father was a professor of the Law School and mother was a writer. In weekends, he cleaned the whole house from the ground level to second floor using the mop and water basket, even if no one told him to do. Minah, I am sure you also would do cleaning diligently in summer vacation like him?"

Minah nodded to her Aunt.

"Oh my! Gen Whitcomb was a really admirable man. How could he be so smart and devoted?" Grandma admired, and Aunt responded saying,

"It came from his rich experiences of career. Gen Whitcomb had fought in the 1st World War, and after the war, he had built a large experiences through working in the government agencies and private enterprises. He was a very promising character enough to be recommended as a candidate of governor, but he decided to participate in the 2nd World War as a rank of colonel. He had commanded the troops in several countries including Iceland, United Kingdom (UK) and France."

"Oh, he was a veteran of many wars. Korean War was not his first time of war participation."

Grandma said, and Aunt nodded to Grandma.

"1944년 6월 6일, 노르망디 상륙작전 때 '오마하 해안 전투'에서 위트컴 대령이 큰 공을 세웠어. 노르망디 작전은 연합군이 유럽을 탈환하는 데 발판을 마련한 최초의 작전이야. 위트컴 대령이 어려운 상황에서 5만여 명의 연합군 병력과 군수물자 수송을 훌륭하게 지휘한 거지. 프랑스 정부에서 위트컴 대령의 눈부신 활약을 치하해 최고 훈장인 제1무공훈장을 수여했대. 제2차 세계대전이 끝난 후 세계 여러 나라에서 중요한 일을 하다가 6·25전쟁 소식을 듣고 우리나라에 온 거지."

민아는 고모의 이야기를 듣고 경험이 정말 중요하다는 것을 깨달았어요.

"그나저나 아침부터 왜 호출했어. 엄마."

고모의 말에 할머니의 표정이 갑자기 어두워졌어요.

"요즘 자꾸 떠오르는 인물이 있어서. 우리 윗집에 살던 나진희라고. 엄마랑 둘이 살았는데 불이 났을 때 그 엄마는 미처 피하지 못한 거 같아. 누가 안고 내려왔는지 진희만 살아남았지. 우리 엄마가 나랑 진희를 같이 재우고 그랬는데, 어느 날 학교 갔다 오니 애가 없는 거야. 그때 다섯 살이었으니 지금 75세일 거야. 찾을 수 있을까?"

"나이와 이름이 정확하다면 뭐 어려운 일은 아니지."

"Colonel Whitcomb made distinguished achievements in Omaha Beach Battle in the Normandy Amphibious Landing Operation conducted in June 1944. That operation was a very critical one to lay a foundation to recapture the lost European regions. He had conducted an excellent command of transporting successfully 50,000 troops and large military logistics overcoming lots of difficulties. French Government awarded him the First Military Meritorious Medal - the highest tier, to praise for his brilliant performance. After the 2nd World War, he performed many important missions, and when he heard the news Korean War broke out, he decided to participate in."

Minah once again realized the importance of the experience from her Aunt's mentioning.

"By the way, what brings you to call me from the early morning, Mom?"

By Aunt's asking, Grandma's faces suddenly became dark and said,

"Recently, an image of a girl frequently comes to my mind. Her name was Jinhee who had lived next to my house. She lived only with her mother, and the day when the big fire broke out, her mother seemed not be able to escape from the house. Fortunately, Jinhee could be survived by the hand of some unknown man. Thereafter, my mom used to put me and Jinhee to sleep together, but one day, Jinhee was found missing when I returned from school. She was five years old at that time, may be 75 now if she is alive. Is it possible to find her?

"Of course, Mom. It might not be a problem to find her if we have her right name and correct birth year."

할머니의 얼굴이 그제야 환하게 펴졌어요.

"오늘 메리놀병원에 한 번 가보자.

위트컴 장군님 도움으로 지은 병원이니 민아도 가봐야지."

할머니의 부탁에 고모가 일어났어요. 할머니 집과 가까워 고모 자동차로 금방 도착했어요. 할머니와 고모와 함께 병원 안으로 들어가는데 복도 벽에 메리놀병원 역사를 담은 안내판이 있었어요. 고모가 손가락으로 짚으며 설명해줬어요.

"제일 위에 메리놀수녀의원 사진있네.

바로 아래 3층 건물이 위트컴 장군님 도움으로 지은 병원이고."

작은 메리놀수녀의원이 메리놀종합병원이 되었다가 지금의 대형 병원으로 발전한 건 정말 놀라운 일이에요.

"위트컴 장군님이 메리놀병원만 도운 줄 알았는데 침례병원, 성분도병원, 복음병원, 독일적십자병원 짓는 일도 지원했대. 1960년대 초반까지만 해도 부산의 의료 수준이 전국에서 가장 높았다잖아."

고모의 말에 할머니가 "세상에나, 어떻게 그 많은 일을……"이라며 말을 잇지 못했어요.

Grandma's face then brightened up to hear Aunt's positive answer, and she said, "O.K, let's visit Maryknoll Hospital today. Minah should go with us because it was built by the full support of Gen Whitcomb.

Aunt stood up, and she drove us to the Maryknoll Hospital. We arrived shortly because the Hospital was very near from my Grandma's house. When we entered the Hospital, we saw the information board in the lobby showing the history of this Hospital, and Aunt explained it using her fingers.

"Let's look at the picture of Maryknoll Sisters' Clinic on top. Just below it, the three store building is the hospital which was built by the support of Gen Whitcomb."

It is amazing to see the history that a small Maryknoll Sister's Hospital was expanded to Maryknoll Hospital, and finally to the current large General Hospital.

"We are surprised to find out that Gen Whitcomb supported the building of not only Maryknoll Hospital, but also Baptist Hospital, St. Benedict Hospital, Evangelical Hospital, and German Red Cross Hospital. In early 1960, the medical level of Busan was renowned as the highest in Korea.

부산대의 미래와 한국 청년의 도약을 위해

다음 날 고모가 부산대학교에 가보자고 했어요.

"요즘 위트컴 위트컴 노래를 부르면서도 부산대 얘기를 안 하는 거 보면 엄마가 잘 모르는 것 같아서. 부산대학교 초창기에 위트컴 장군님이 많이 도와주셨지."

할머니가 "너하고 민아 애비가 다닌 학교잖아. 세상에나, 훌륭도 하시지"라며 또 탄복했어요. 고모가 운전하고 가면서 자세한 설명을 해주었어요.

부산대는 단과대학으로 개교했다가 1953년에 종합대학으로 승격했어. 윤인구 초대 총장님은 아직 땅도 없는데 장차 조성될 학교를 상상하며 기도했대. 미국 프린스턴 신학대학원에 다닐 때 눈여겨봤던 학교 풍경을 참고해 배치도까지 그려놓고 말야.

1954년 6월 8일 위트컴 장군님이 부산대를 방문하자 윤 총장님은 배치도를 꺼내 대학 본관, 대학극장, 도서관, 운동장, 강의동에 대해 열심히 설명했지. 위트컴 장군님은 짜임새 있게 배치한 그림을 찬찬히 살펴보며 열심히 들었어.

"우리 학교는 작년에 종합대학으로 승격했지만 부지를 구하지 못한 데다 건립 자금 마련도 힘들어 애로를 겪고 있습니다. 부산대의 미래를 위해, 대한민국 청년의 도약을 위해 투자해주세요. 교육에 대한 제 꿈을 사주세요." 위트컴 장군님은 진심을 다해 부탁하는 윤 총장님의 태도에 감동해 고개를 끄덕였어.

For the future of Pusan National University (PNU) as well as the Rise of the young generations in Korea

Pusan National University (PNU) began as a college in its initial stage and later promoted to the University in 1953. Dr. Yoon, Ingoo, the first president of the University, prayed God for the development of the University which would be newly built. Although he actually had no land available for the project of building, nevertheless, he even portrayed the layout of the future university referring to the landscape of the Princeton Theological Seminary where he studied. When Gen Whitcomb happen to visit the University, Dr. Yoon showed him a layout he portrayed and ardently explained him about the main section of the buildings, theater, playground, stadium, and lecture halls, etc. Gen Whitcomb listened to him earnestly and carefully scrutinized his well-structured layout.

"General, Pusan college was fortunately promoted to University last year, but we are facing lots of difficulties of land and budget. I would entreat you to invest for the future of PNU and young generations in Korea. Please buy my dream of the education."

Gen Whitcomb was deeply impressed by and nodded to Dr. Yoon for his earnest request.

"할 수 있는 한 열심히 돕겠습니다. 교육은 가장 중요한 가치입니다. 당신의 노력을 존중합니다."

그 말에 힘입어 열심히 땅을 물색하던 윤 총장님이 얼마 후 위트컴 장군님에게 연락했어.

"금정산 기슭에 있는 일본인 농장에 학교를 지으면 좋겠습니다."

윤 총장님은 위트컴 장군님에게 땅의 위치와 크기에 대해 자세히 설명했어.

위트컴 장군님은 바로 경남도지사와 이승만 대통령을 만나 대한민국의 미래를 담당할 인재 양성을 위해 학교를 지어야 한다고 간곡하게 설득했어. 그렇게 해서 165만 2,892m²나 되는 장전동 부지가 부산대에 무상으로 제공되었어. 땅이 마련되자 위트컴 장군님은 약속대로 AFAK 기금으로 부산대에 25만 달러 상당의 건축 자재를 지원했어.

"I would be glad to help you as possible as I can. I think the education is the most important value, and I pay my respect for your great endeavors."

Encouraged by his good words, Dr. Yoon exerted all his efforts to search the proper land site, and finally found it and gave him a call.

"I think I found the good and proper site. It is the old Japanese farmstead located near by the mountainous area of Kumjeongsan."

Dr. Yoon met with Gen Whitcomb and explained in detail the exact location and size of the land. Then Gen Whitcomb immediately met with the Governor of Kyungnam Province and President Rhee, Syngman, thus persuaded them to build the university for the future of the promising young generations of Korea. Therefore, it consequently concluded that the land of 1,652,892 square meters (0.5 million Pyung) located in Jang jeondong was provided to PNU as free. Gen Whitcomb also supported the large amount of construction supplies equivalent to 0.25 million dollars as he promised.

위트컴 장군님이 버스 종점에서부터 부산대 무지개문까지 1.6km 길도 닦아주었어. 1950년대는 포장된 도로가 거의 없었어. 전차나 버스에서 내린 학생들이 편하게 올라가라고 길을 닦아준 거야. 미군 434 공병부대가 길을 만들고 부지 정리도 해주고 공과대학 건물도 지어주었지.

"세상에나, 위트컴 장군님이 부산대학교도 도와주셨구나. 이 은혜를 어찌 다 갚을고."

잔뜩 감동한 할머니를 보며 민아도 위트컴 장군님이 점점 더 좋아졌어요. 여기저기 열심히 살펴봤지만 학교가 너무 커서 다 볼 수 없었어요. 다음에 또 오기로 하고 돌아왔어요.

그날 저녁 TV에서 위트컴 장군님 동상 모금액이 다 채워졌다는 뉴스가 나왔어요. 할머니는 "세상에나, 정말 잘됐다. 다행이다"라며 좋아했어요.

원래 1년 동안 모금할 계획이었는데 7개월 만에 1만 8,300여 명이 3억 6,500만 원의 성금을 내서 마감한다는 소식이었어요.

"와, 우리 부산 시민들 의리 있다. 멋있다. 11월에 동상 개막식을 한다고 했지? 우리 그때 가보자."

할머니의 말에 민아도 꼭 가보고 싶었어요.

Moreover, he paved the road of 1.6 km long from the bus stop to the Rainbow Gate of the University. There were seldom paved roads in the decade of 1950 in Busan, and it was vert good for the students to easily come and go from the bus stop to school. The 434th US Engineer Corps made the roads, cleared the sites and constructed the buildings of College of Engineering.

"Oh, my God! Gen Whitcomb even supported the PNU! How can we repay him of his favour?"

Minah became to be fond of Gen Whitcomb more and more, feeling Grandma deeply impressed. Since the University was too large to look around every corner and corner, they returned home promising to visit again.

That evening, TV aired the news that the fundraising project for the statue was successfully accomplished. Grandma was very delighted to hear the news, saying "Oh, my, it is really good, God's blessing." The fundraising project was originally designed to raise 300 million won within a year, but could be successfully completed within only seven month raising 365million won donated by 18,300 Busan citizens.

"Wow, our credible friends of Busan! Great! Is it November to have opening ceremony of the Statue? We then go to see the ceremony."

Minah really wanted to go and join the ceremony with Grandma.

한국유엔기념공원에 잠든 유일한 장성

오늘은 위트컴 장군님이 잠든 한국유엔기념공원에 가기로 했어요. 분홍색을 즐겨 입는 할머니가 검정색 옷을 입었어요. 참배하러 가는 거니까 예의를 차려야 한다는 말에 민아도 부랴부랴 검정색으로 갈아입었어요. 고모도 검정색 옷을 입고 왔어요. 자동차를 타는데 뒷좌석에 흰국화 다발이 놓여 있었어요.

"유엔기념공원은 세계 유일의 유엔군 묘지이자 성지야. 6·25전쟁 때 유엔군 4만여 명이 희생되셨는데 유엔기념공원에 11개국의 2,320분을 안장했어. 그때 미군이 가장 많이 돌아가셨으나 3만 6,492구의 유해를 모두 미국으로 모셔갔대."

고모의 설명에 할머니가 걱정스러운 목소리로 말했어요.

"위트컴 장군님도 미국인인데 유엔기념공원에 계신 거 맞냐?"

"염려마슈. 휴전 후 한국에 주둔해있던 미군 중에서 한국에 안장되기를 희망한 40분이 유엔기념공원에 잠들어 계시니까.

2,320분 가운데 한 분만 빼고 모두 사병이야. 별을 단 분은 위트컴 장군님뿐이래. 유엔기념공원에 잠든 분 가운데 가장 계급이 높으시지."

고모의 말에 할머니가 "참 겸손도 하시지"라고 했어요.

The only general buried in the United Nations Memorial Cemetery in Korea (UNMCK)

Today we planned to visit UNMCK. Grandma was dressed in black today instead of her favorite pinky color. Minah also hurried to change her dress in black following Grandma's advice that keeping politeness to pay tribute and honor be important for the ceremony. Aunt was dressed in black, too. As we got in the car, we saw a bouquet of white chrysanthemum laid in the back seat.

"UNMCK is an unique UN Memorial Cemetery as well as a sanctuary in the world. Approximately 40,000 UN forces were sacrificed in Korean War, and among them, 2,320 from 11 countries were buried here. American soldiers were the most in numbers, but 36,492 remains were repatriated to their country.

Grandma asked Aunt in concerned voice, "Is Gen Whitcomb surely sleeping here? He is an American, isn't he?" Aunt answered, "Don't worry, mom. Among American victims, 40 were buried here and Gen Whitcomb, too. Among 2,320 who were buried here, all is enlisted except Gen Whitcomb. He is an only general and the highest rank among the victims buried here "

"How humble man he is!" Grandma responded to Aunt.

한국유엔기념공원에 도착해 추모 동영상을 봤어요. 민아는 6·25전쟁과 유엔기념공원의 역사에 대해 열심히 들었어요. 세계 각국의 청년들이 자유를 위해 귀한 희생 치른 것에 민아는 큰 고마움을 느꼈어요. 묘역으로 가기 전 안내원이 묘지에 들어가면 안 된다고 했어요. 길을 닦아 놓았으니 그쪽으로만 조용히 다니라고 당부했어요. 남의 묘에 함부로 들어가는 건 고인은 물론 유족에게 실례가 되기 때문이죠. 할머니는 고개를 끄덕이면서도 안타까운 표정을 지었어요. 고모는 핸드폰으로 미국 묘역을 검색해 위트컴 장군님의 묘 위치를 파악했어요.

As we arrived at UNMCK, we watched the memorial video. Minah listened carefully about the 6.25 War and the history of UNMCK. She felt grateful for the sacrifices of the young men and women dispatched from the whole world. The tour guide advised us not to get in the private grave and asked us to get along the paved road quietly. It would be also out of the manner to get in others' grave. Grandma nodded but with pitiful face. Aunt searched the exact location of Gen Whitcomb's grave using her mobile phone.

"미국 묘역이 주묘역의 맨아래쪽인 데다 위트컴 장군님이 두 번째 줄에 계셔서 안으로 들어가지 않고도 잘 보일 것 같아. 엄마, 꽃은 보여드리고 마음으로 바치면 되지."

고모의 말에 할머니가 고개를 끄덕였어요.

대리석으로 만든 사각 관문을 통과하자 정갈하게 가꾼 묘역이 보였어요.

이름과 국적을 새긴 동판을 받치고 있는 묘비석과 반듯반듯하게 다듬은 키 작은 나무가 마치 사열하듯 줄을 맞춰 서 있었어요.

우리나라를 위해 귀한 목숨 바친 분들 생각에 민아의 고개가 저절로 숙여졌어요.

고모의 안내에 따라 주묘역에 있는 미군 묘지로 갔어요.

"엄마, 오늘 위트컴 장군님도 뵙고 아주 큰 선물도 기다리고 있으니 기대해."

고모의 말에 할머니가 어리둥절한 표정을 지었어요.

고모가 안내한 위트컴 장군님 묘지는 묘비석과 사각으로 깎은 작은 나무 한 그루뿐이었어요. 훌륭한 장군님이 사병들과 함께 소박하게 묻혀 있다는 사실이 정말 감동적이었어요.

최대한 가까이 가서 위트컴 장군님의 묘지를 바라봤어요.

할머니는 국화꽃을 들고 눈을 감았어요. 민아도 눈을 감고 마음속으로 말했어요.

"장군님 고마워요. 순이가 따뜻하게 지낼 수 있도록 텐트를 쳐주시고 이재민 주택을 지어주셔서 고마워요. 메리놀병원 짓는 일과 아빠와 고모가 다닌 부산대학교를 도와주신 일, 모두 감사해요."

"The American sector is located in the bottom area from the main cemetery. As Gen Whitcomb is buried in the second line, we could easily identify his grave. Mom, we don't have to get in his grave, instead, just show him the flower and lay a wreath with our heart."

Grandma nodded to Aunt. The neatly managed tomb was seen through the square-angled gate which was made of marble. The tombstones supporting the copper plates which were engraved in victim's name and nationality, and the small trees trimmed straight and straight stood as if they were in review for inspection. Minah automatically bowed to pay honour for their valuable sacrifices in Korea.

Aunt guided us to American sector in the main lot.

"Mom, today, we meet with Gen Whitcomb, and you may guess a big gift for you."

Grandma made a bewildered facial expression against Aunt.

Aunt guided us to the grave of Gen Whitcomb. His grave looked simple with a gravestone and a small tree trimmed squared. It was very impressive to see the admirable general who was plainly buried with the enlisted men and women.

Minah approached closer and saw the General's grave. Grandma closed her eyes holding the chrysanthemum bouquet. Minah also closed her eyes and whispered herself in mind.

"Thank you General for setting a tent for Sooni to keep her warm, building houses for the refugees, supporting the building of Maryknoll Hospital and the Busan University where my Father and Aunt went. Thank you for all."

민아가 눈을 떴을 때 흰색 정장 차림에 꽃다발을 든 분이 다가오고 있었어요.

"나진희 선생님이신가요?"

고모의 말에 그분이 "네"라고 하자 할머니가 "어허헝"하고 털버덕 주저앉았어요.

"언니, 순이 언니. 저 진희예요."

할머니와 나진희 선생님이 끌어안고 엉엉 울었어요. 민아는 그제야 고모가 '큰 선물이 있다'라고 한 말이 생각났어요. 나진희 선생님은 눈물을 닦은 후 길 위에서 위트컴 장군님 묘를 향해 절을 두 번 올렸어요.

"언니, 매년 위트컴 장군님 기일 때 같이 와요."

"그러면 우리가 일 년에 한 번은 만나겠네."

할머니와 나진희 선생님이 두 손을 잡고 기뻐했어요. 하지만 눈에는 눈물이 홍건했어요.

As Minah opened her eyes, a lady in full dress holding a bouquet was approaching to us.

"Excuse me, are you teacher Ms. Na, Jinhee?" Aunt asked her, and the lady answered "Yes!", then my Grandma flopped down with sighing "Ah, Hung…".

"Sister Sooni, it's me. Jinhee~"

Grandma and Jinhee embraced together and loudly cried. Minah only then recognized Aunt's mentioning of the big gift for Grandma. Ms. Na cleared her eyes and gave two polite bows toward the General's grave from the roadside.

"Sister Sooni, How about coming here on his date of death every year?"

"That's good, then we can meet each other at least once a year."

Grandma and Ms. Na, overjoyed holding their hands in hands, but their eyes were heavily soaked up.

한국 고아의 아버지

나진희 선생님은 할머니댁에서 하루 묵기로 했어요.

나진희 선생님 손자가 인스타그램에 가족 소식을 자주 올리며 해시태그를 착실히 달아 고모가 쉽게 찾을 수 있었어요. 중학교 선생님으로 재직하다 퇴직했다는 나진희 선생님의 말에 할머니가 "장하다"라며 좋아했어요.

"언니가 학교 갈 때 따라 나갔다가 길을 잃어 헤맸던 것 같아.

그다음에 어디론가 실려 갔고 거기서 여러 아이와 지내다 충남 천안에 있는 고아원에 들어갔어.

내가 살았던 익선원은 우리나라 최초의 고아원이야. 나에게 행운의 집이었지."

익선원의 한묘숙 원장님은 언제나 아이들에게 깨끗한 옷을 입히고 배불리 먹였대요.

"어느 날 미국 아저씨가 먹을 거랑 옷을 잔뜩 갖고 오셨어.

그때 위트컴 장군님을 처음 뵈었어."

"무슨 소리야. 위트컴 장군님이 텐트촌에 자주 오셨는데 기억 안 나?"

"정말? 불이 났고 텐트에서 언니하고 지낸 건 기억나는데 다른 건 잘 모르겠어.

내가 다섯 살 때도 위트컴 장군님의 도움을 받았다니, 놀라워."

The father of Korean orphans

Ms. Na, Jinhee wished to stay at Grandma's house for one day. As her grandson frequently posted his family news on his Instagram with stable hash-tag, so Aunt could easily find Ms. Na using this access. Ms. Na had taught in middle school and now retired. Grandma was very delighted to hear from Jinhee and said "Great! my dear."

"I seemed to be lost during the time when I followed your school going. I seemed to be taken to some place, stayed there with some friends, and finally went to orphanage in Chonan city, Chungcheong Namdo. The orphanage where I lived was Iksonwon, and it was the first orphanage established in Korea. It was a house of luck to me."

She said that Ms. Han, Myosook, the director of Iksonwon, always treated the kids well dressed and good meal.

"One day, an American gentleman visited my orphanage carrying a big amount of the clothes and food. It was my first time to meet Gen Whitcomb."

"First time? What are you talking about now? Gen Whitcomb frequently visited our tent camp. Don't you remember it?"

"Really? I could only remember the time spending with you in tent, but I don't remember anything else. It is amazing that the General helped me even at my age of five."

위트컴 장군님은 퇴역 이후 이승만 대통령의 정치고문을 맡아 미국 백악관과 연락하는 업무를 하면서 부산의 발전을 도왔대요.

위트컴 장군님이 미국에 돌아가지 않은 진짜 이유는 전쟁고아를 돕고 싶어서였다고 해요. 민간단체인 한미재단까지 만들어 전국의 많은 고아원을 도운 위트컴 장군님의 별명이 '한국 고아의 아버지'였대요.

Gen Whitcomb retired from the US Army and became a political advisor to President Rhee, Syngman. He performed his mission keeping the communication with the White House, and besides, supported the development of Busan.

The real reason why Gen Whitcomb didn't return to his country America and remained in Korea was that he wished to help the war orphans. As his nick name ' 'Father of Korean orphans' indicated, he helped lots of Korean orphans through the private civil organization 'Korea America Foundation' which he had established by himself.

"위트컴 장군님이 도움을 준 고아원을 다시 방문해 보면 아이들이 여전히 꾀죄죄한 옷을 그대로 입은 채 배를 곯고 있었대. 그런데 익선원 아이들은 예쁜 옷을 입은 데다 통통하게 살아 올라있었지. 우리 원장님은 후원금이나 후원 물품을 아이들을 위해 다 쓰셨어. 정직한 우리 원장님이 아이들을 진정으로 사랑하는 걸 보신 위트컴 장군님이 청혼을 하셨어."

"위트컴 장군님이 결혼을 하셨다고?"

"네, 언니. 한묘숙 원장님이 사실은 대단한 집안의 따님이셨어. 이혼하고 두 아이를 키우며 우리를 성심껏 돌보다가 좋은 분을 만난 거지."

"위트컴 장군님이 원장님보다 서른한 살 많았어. 원장님이 존경을 담아 늘 '위트컴 장군님'이라고 하셔서 우리도 그렇게 불렀지. 위트컴 장군님이 우리를 사랑해주시고 좋은 말씀도 해주셨어. '어려운 문제가 생겨도 스트레스 느끼지 말라. 이겨내려고 노력하다 보면 능력이 개발되고 점점 어려운 문제를 해결할 수 있게 된다'라는 말이 기억에 남아."

고모는 위트컴 장군님의 말씀을 수첩에 메모했어요.

"Some of the orphanages managed by the support of Gen Whitcomb was found unreliabilities, for example, the kids were in shabby dressed or looked suffering from hunger. Nothing unchanged there in spite of his support. But Iksonwon was quite different. The kids were dressed in good clothes and looked chubby. It's because of the honest use of the donation money and good management of director Ms. Han, Myosook. She spent all of donation money and resources fully for the orphans. Honest Ms. Han's true loving for the orphans led Gen Whitcomb to decide to propose her the marriage.

"What? Did you say that Gen Whitcomb got married?"

"Yes, Sister Sooni. Ms. Han, in fact, was a daughter of a renowned family. She was once divorced but sincerely devoted her life for taking care of the orphans like me while simultaneously raising her two kids. Then, she luckly met with a good person."

"Gen Whitcomb was at that time 31 years older than Ms. Han. As Director Han always called him respectfully 'Gen Whitcomb!', so we did call him same as Ms. Han did. The General also loved us much, always telling us good words. One of his famous sayings, 'Do not be distressed when you face the difficulties. if you try harder to overcome them, your capability would be developed more, and you can gradually fix them up by yourself~~' has been still kept in my memory."

Aunt took a note for the words of Gen Whitcomb.

"위트컴 장군님은 세 가지를 평생의 교훈으로 삼았어. 첫째, 염려하지 말라. 대부분 별 의미없는 걱정이다. 둘째, 옳은 일이라면 즉시 행동하라. 윤리적 기준에 부합하면 망설이지 말고 과감하게 나서라. 셋째, 옳다고 믿으면 굽히지 말라. 본질적 가치를 포기하면 의미가 사라진다. 나도 그 말을 늘 기억하며 실천하려고 애썼어."

나진희 선생님의 말이 끝나자 할머니가 질문했어요.

"위트컴 장군님 뵈러 올 때 왜 꽃다발을 두 개 갖고 온 거야?"

"아까 그 묘지에 두 분이 같이 계셔. 한묘숙 원장님이 남편과 함께 묻히고 싶어 유엔기념공원에 요청해 승인을 받았어. 2017년 1월 1일 하늘나라로 가시면서 함께 잠들게 됐지."

할머니와 나진희 선생님은 두 분이 같이 계셔서 정말 좋다고 했어요.

"Gen Whitcomb kept three lessons in his whole life. First, don't get worried. Most of your worries are meaningless. Second, act promptly if you think it right. Don't hesitate and go straight boldly if you think it meets ethical standards. Last, don't give up if you think it right. If you abandon the intrinsic value, the essence of the meaning disappears. I tried to remember and practice these words in my life."

After Ms. Na's saying, Grandma asked Ma. Na " Why do you bring two bunches of bouquet?"

Ms. Na answered, "It is because Gen Whitcomb and his wife Ms. Han are buried here together. Ms. Han requested UNMCK of burying together and it was approved. She passed away 1st Jan 2017 and now sleeping with her husband."

Grandma and Ms. Na said in one voice that it is really good for the couple being together.

장진호에서 싸운 미 해병을 기억하라

밤늦은 시각까지 두 분의 대화는 그칠 줄 몰랐어요.

"바쁘다는 핑계로 한묘숙 원장님 살아생전에 뵙지 못해 죄송하지. 검색을 하다가 2011년에 시사잡지 '신동아' 기자가 한묘숙 원장님과 인터뷰한 기사를 읽었어. 정말 감동적인 내용이었어. 그 기사를 보니 위트컴 장군님이 한국에 남은 또하나 중요한 이유가 있었어. 장진호 전투에서 사망한 미군 해병대원의 유해를 찾기 위해서였지."

나진희 선생님이 핸드폰을 꺼내 무언가를 찾더니 할머니에게 보여줬어요.

"이 동영상을 보고 얼마나 울었는지 몰라."

나진희 선생님이 내민 장면은 눈이 많이 내리는 산에서 미군들이 걸어가는 모습이었어요.

"함경남도 개마고원 장진호에서 전투가 벌어졌을 때 기온이 영하 40도였대. 그 추운 곳에서 우리나라를 위해 유엔군이 중공군과 전투하다가 많이 돌아가셨대. 너무도 가슴 아프고, 너무도 감사하고, 너무도 미안해."

눈을 맞으며 걷는 병사들이 가마니 같은 걸 끌고 가는 모습도 보였어요.

Remember the US Marines who fought in Chosin Reservoir (Jangjinho)

The conversation between two ladies continued to later night.

"I felt deeply sorry for seldom visit to Ms. Han while she was alive, just having the excuse of being busy. I once read the article of the some reporter's interview with Ms. Han in Shindonga magazine. The article was so impressive. In that interview, I found another reason why Gen Whitcomb remained in Korea. It was his desire to find out the remains of the dead US Marines who fought in Chosin Reservoir.

Ms. Na took out her mobile phone and showed something to my Grandma.

"I wept so much to see this video."

The scene Ms. Na showed was that US Marines was miserably walking down from the snowy mountain.

"The weather was recorded -40 degree centigrade in Chosin Reservoir battle area on Gaemagowon, Hamkyung Namdo. Too many UN forces were killed in action by the Chinese Communist Army to defend Korea. I felt very sorry and heart breaking, but grateful for them."

Some soldiers was walking in the snow drawing the straw mats.

"전사한 병사들을 산 아래로 옮기는 장면이야. 추운 날씨에 마음까지 얼어붙었을 병사들 생각에 가슴이 너무 아파."

나진희 선생님이 독백하듯 장진호 전투에 대해 들려주었어요.

1950년 11월 27일부터 12월 11일까지 유엔군 3만 명과 중공군 12만 명이 격돌한 장진호 전투를 꼭 기억해야 해. 미 제10군단 예하 미 해병 제1사단이 주축이 된 유엔군이 중공군의 포위망을 뚫고 흥남에 도착하기까지 2주간 전개한 철수 작전이야. 장진호 전투는 강추위와 험난한 지형, 겹겹이 쌓인 적의 포위망을 돌파한 역사상 가장 성공한 전투로 평가받고 있어.

장진호 전투에서 병사들이 많이 희생됐으나 유해를 다 찾지 못했대. 미국과 북한이 합의하여 몇 차례 유해 찾는 일을 하다가 중단되자 위트컴 장군님이 굉장히 애석해하셨대. 며칠을 마음 아파하신 장군님이 혼자서라도 해병대원의 유해를 찾아 미국 품에 안기기로 결심하셨대.

"The scene showed carrying the dead bodies down from the mountains. I felt very sad to think of the frozen soldiers physically and mentally.

Ms. Na told us the story of Chosin Reservoir Battle as she seemed to speak to herself.

The Battle of Chosin Reservoir which was conducted from 27th Nov to 11th Dec 1950 between 30,000 UN Forces and 120,000 Chinese Communist Army should not be forgotten. The battle was the retreat operations of the UN Forces (mainly consisted of The 1st US Marine Division under the US 10th Army Corps) penetrating the envelopment circle of the Chinese Communist Army and marched toward Hungnam port. The battle was estimated as one of the most successful retreat operation in war history overcoming the inclement weather of bitter coldness, terribly rugged terrain and several nets of enemy's envelopment circle.

Too many casualties were sacrificed in the Chosin Reservoir Battle, but the dead remains were not recovered all. As US and NK jointly agreed and worked several times in finding the remains, but failed to continue, Gen Whitcomb was very regrettable. After spending several days of heart breaking, he decided to recover the remains of US Marines and to repatriate them to America by himself.

북한에 가려면 중국을 통과해야 해. 우리나라와 중국은 1992년에야 정식 수교를 맺었으니 그전에는 홍콩이나 타이완을 통해야 중국에 갈 수 있었어. 위트컴 장군님은 알려진 사람이어서 직접 갈 수 없었지. 대신 세계 여러 나라에서 쌓은 인맥을 총동원해 아내를 보냈어. 한묘숙 원장님이 홍콩과 타이완을 100번도 넘게 드나들며 방법을 찾다가 1979년에야 홍콩 사업가의 초청으로 중국 본토에 들어갔어.

한묘숙 원장님이 중국에서 살다시피 하며 북한에 갈 방도를 찾고 있을 때 서울에서 슬픈 소식이 들려왔어. 1982년 7월 12일, 88세의 나이로 위트컴 장군님이 하늘나라에 가신 거야. 위트컴 장군님은 미군들에게 빌려주는 작은방에서 월세를 내고 소박하게 사셨대. 아내가 중국을 오가는 데 많은 돈이 들었기 때문이지. 원장님은 중국 베이징에서 북한 측 인사와 만나다가 소식을 듣고 급히 귀국했어. 원장님은 가족과 친지들만 모인 조촐한 장례식에서 위트컴 장군님이 평소 유언처럼 했던 말을 되새겼어.

"6·25전쟁 때 죽어간 미군 유해를 꼭 고향으로 보내달라. 나를 제2의 고향인 부산의 유엔기념공원에 묻어달라."

소원대로 위트컴 장군님은 한국유엔기념공원에 안장되었어.

At that time, the entry to NK was only available thru China, but it was impossible because the diplomatic relations between Korea and China was not established yet, later made in 1992. So the entry to NK was only possible through Taiwan or Hong Kong. As Gen Whitcomb was so renowned person that he couldn't go to NK by himself, instead, he decided to send his wife Ms. Han to NK mobilizing all of his connection network around the world. Ms. Han visited Hong Kong and Taiwan more than hundred times to seek the way of access to NK, and she finally grabbed the chance to enter the mainland of China in 1979 by the invitation of a Hong Kong business man.

While Ms. Han stayed in China as if permanent residency struggling to find the way of passage to NK, a sad news flew from Seoul that Gen Whitcomb passed away on 12th July 1982 at the age of 88. Gen Whitcomb had to live naively in a small shelter which was allowed to US military personnel paying monthly rent, because he poured a big expenses for Ms. Han's NK mission. Ms. Han hastily returned to Korea to hear the news suspending the meeting with a certain NK person. In small funeral service attended by few family members and friends, she reiterated in her mind of Gen Whitcomb's consistent words like a will,

"Please do your best to repatriate the dead remains of the US soldiers to their home. and bury me in UNMCK, my second home Busan.

Per his wish, Gen Whitcomb was buried in UNMCK.

마미를 부르며 하늘나라로 간 미군들

위트컴 장군님이 돌아가셨다는 말에 할머니가 눈물 지었어요. 할머니가 슬퍼하는 모습에 민아의 마음도 울적했어요.

"언니, 위트컴 장군님 나이가 88세였어. 아쉽지만 그래도 오래 사셨으니까 슬퍼하지 마. 좋은 일 많이 하셨으니 하늘나라에서 편히 쉬고 계실 거야. 위트컴 장군님이 돌아가신 뒤 우리 원장님이 고생하셨지."

나진희 선생님이 한숨을 푸 내쉬면서 이야기를 이어갔어요.

남편이 세상을 떠난 후에도 한묘숙 원장님은 계속 북한에 갈 방법을 모색했어. 1989년, 허담 북한 조국평화통일위원장의 초청장이 왔고 1990년 6월 드디어 북한 땅을 밟았어.

원장님이 북한에서 돌아와 김포공항에 내리자마자 국가안전기획부의 조사를 받았대. 원장님이 미국 시민권자인 데다 미국 장군의 부인 신분이어서 사흘 만에 풀려났지. 한묘숙 원장님은 남편의 뜻을 받들어 1990년부터 9년 동안 북한을 스물다섯 번이나 방문했어.

The US soldiers who went to Heaven calling ~ Mommies

Grandma shed the tears to hear that Gen Whitcomb had passed away. Minah also felt depressed with Grandma's sad look.

"Sister Sooni, Gen Whitcomb was at 88 when he passed away. It was a pity, but he had lived his life well, so please don't be sad. The General would sleep peacefully in Heaven. However, Ms. Han lived a harder life after his death."

Ms. Na sighed deeply and continued to speak.

Ms. Han continued to seek the way of entry to NK even after her husband's death and in 1989, she finally had an invitation from Mr. Hur, Dam-North Korea Chairman of the Committee for the peaceful unification of the fatherland- and could land NK in June of 1990.

Ms. Han was interrogated by the Agency for National Security Planning (ANSP) soon after she arrived at Kimpo International Airport from NK. Since she had an American citizenship as well as the spouse of US Army general, she could be released after three days. Afterwards, Ms. Han made total 25 visits to NK from 1990 to 1999 to accomplish her husbands' will.

탈북자나 조선족이 미군 유해에서 나온 도그 태그(Dog Tag·군번줄)를 찾아오면 500~1,000달러를 지급했어. 300개의 군번줄을 받았는데 대부분 가짜였대. 간혹 미군 유해라며 뼈를 들고 오는 사람도 있었는데 확인해보면 동물 뼈다귀였다는 거야. 돈을 받기 위해 사람들이 거짓말을 한 거지. 속은 걸 알고도 원장님은 그들을 나무라지 않으셨어. 싫은 소리를 하면 다음에 가져오지 않을까 봐 그랬던 거지.

 유해가 발굴되면 판문점까지 가져오게 한 뒤 미군의 '전쟁포로 및 실종자 확인 합동사령부(JPAC)'에 전했대. 그러면 미 국방부 산하의 '전쟁포로·실종자 사무국(DPMO)'에서 사망·실종자 명단과 맞춰보고 친인척 유전자 감식을 통해 진위 밝히는 작업을 했대. 북한에서 가져온 유해 중에 우리 국군의 유해도 있었다니 다행한 일이지.

 북한을 오가는 한묘숙 원장님에게 간첩 누명을 씌우고 "미친 사람, 이중 스파이, 대북 로비스트"라며 음해하는 사람도 있었대. 하지만 원장님은 굴하지 않고 남편의 유지를 받들었어.

 한묘숙 원장님은 북한에 들어갈 때마다 옷이나 심장약 등 의약품을 몇 상자씩 준비해서 가셨어. 선물을 준비하지 않으면 북한에 쉽게 들어갈 수 없었겠지. 돈이 많이 들어 서울 집을 팔고 물려받은 재산을 다 썼대. 위트컴 장군님의 연금도 다 쏟아부었고. 결혼식 때 받은 패물까지 팔아야 했어. 30년간 남편의 유지를 받느라 전 재산을 다 바쳤어.

The dog-tags (military service number) found from the remains of US soldiers by NK defectors or Korean-Chinese were rewarded 300 US dollars per each. Ms. Han received approximately 300 dog-tags from them, but most of them were confirmed fake. Some carried the animal bond insisting it human one, but it was proved fake too. People lied just for the money, but Ms. Han didn't blame them cause she worried whether they would not bring the dog-tags any more.

Once the remains were recovered, they would be carried to Panmunjom and transmitted to JPAC (Joint POW/MIA Accounting Command), and then DPMO (Defense Prisoner of War/Missing Personnel Office) took the actions to examine it whether fake or not, and worked the task of uncovering the truth through genetic identification of the relatives. Sometimes very few Korean remains were luckly included in the repatriation from NK.

Some people falsely accused Ms. Han that she would be espionage for NK or blamed her as "crazy woman, double agent, pro-NK lobbyist, ... etc, because of her frequent trips to NK, but she consistently perfomed her mission following her husband's will without any inch of waver.

Ms. Han had to bring several boxes of clothes, medical supplies such as the medicine of heart disease whenever she visited NK, if not, she might not enter there. She sold her house in Seoul and spent all the property inherited to her. She even poured all the pension of Gen Whitcomb and sold out her personal ornaments of wedding gifts. Conclusively she devoted all of her property in 30 years to support her husband's will.

원장님 기사를 읽다가 눈물을 펑펑 쏟은 일이 있어. 원장님이 장진호에 여러 번 가셨는데 어느 날 안내하던 북한 사람이 "마미가 무슨 뜻입네까?"하고 물었대. 원장님이 "엄마라는 뜻이에요"라고 했더니 안내원이 "미국놈들이 죽을 때 마미를 외쳤다더니 오마니를 찾은 거로구만"이라고 했대. 그러면서 "미국놈들이 배가 고파서로 오줌을 받아먹었다던데. 여기서 2만 명이 죽었대요"라고 대수롭지 않다는 듯 내뱉는 말에 원장님 가슴이 찢어지는 것 같았대.

아, 정말 너무 마음 아파. 그 추운 곳에서 마지막으로 엄마를 외치며 하늘나라로 간 그 미군 청년들 생각하면……"

I once had heavily shed tears to read the article about her. She had several visits to Chosin Reservoir, and one day a NK tour guide asked her what the word 'Mommy' means. As she answered 'it means Mother', the guide responded her, 'the dying Americans shouted 'Mommy~~' and now I understand it meant their 'Mother'. And he added "the dying Americans were told even to reciprocate their urine against starving. Approximately, 20,000 US soldiers were killed in action here.", and this comment broke my heart.

Ah, it is so pitiful to think the young soldiers who went to Heaven crying 'Mommy~~' in bitter coldness……"

나진희 선생님과 할머니가 손수건으로 두 눈을 가리고 흐느껴 울었어요. 미군 병사들이 "엄마!"를 외치며 하늘나라로 갔다는 말에 민아도 눈물이 주르르 흘렀어요. 민아의 얼굴을 닦아주던 고모의 눈도 빨갛게 되었어요.

"유엔군이 온몸으로 막아 중공군의 남하가 2주간 늦어지면서 미군과 한국군 장병, 피란민 20만 명이 남쪽으로 올 수 있었다는 걸 꼭 기억해야 돼. 장진호 전투에서 끝까지 저항하며 싸운 유엔군 덕분에 흥남부두에서 미군 배가 군인들과 피란민을 남쪽으로 실어나를 수 있었어."

나진희 선생님의 말에 할머니가 갑자기 거실 바닥을 치며 울기 시작했어요. 민아는 너무도 슬피우는 할머니의 등을 쓰다듬다가 흥남부두에서 순이가 부모님과 미군 배를 타고 남쪽으로 왔다는 게 떠올랐어요.

"그날 얼마나 추웠다고. 내복에다 솜옷을 입고 두꺼운 담요를 둘둘 감았는 데도 바람이 얼마나 차가운지 바늘로 살을 찌르는 것 같았어. 어린 군인들이 얼마나 추웠을고. 그분들이 목숨을 바친 덕분에 우리가 살았다니, 으흐흑"

할머니의 통곡에 또다시 울음바다가 되었어요.

"장진호에서 목숨 바쳐 싸운 병사들, 우리를 남쪽으로 싣고 온 미군 배, 불이 나서 오갈 데 없는 우리에게 텐트와 이재민 주택을 마련해주신 위트컴 장군님, 이 은혜를 어찌 다 갚을고. 나는 살 날이 많지 않으니 너희가 오래오래 살면서 다 갚아라."

할머니의 말에 고모와 민아는 고개를 힘차게 끄덕였어요.

Ms. Na and Grandma were drowned in tears covering their eyes with handkerchiefs. Minah also felt that the tears falling down her cheeks. Aunt's eyes also became flushed as she cleaned Minah's face.

"We should remember that 200,000 of US/Korean Combined Forces including many war refugees could escape to South due to the successful defense of UN Forces for two weeks. It caused 2 weeks delay of Chinese Communist Army's advance to south. making possible for military troops and war refugees to be evacuated safely to the south."

Grandma started to cry slapping the floor of living room to hear from Ms. Na. While Minah stroked Grandma on her back, suddenly it came across her mind that young girl Sooni escaped to south from Hungnam Port with her parent boarded on the US Navy ship.

"It was terribly cold on that day. We wore the padded clothes with underwears, put the heavy blanket around the body, but the cold and strong wind seemed to penetrate us like needle. What a pitiful young soldiers in coldness ~~! Our lives indebted to their sacrifices, Huu~~"

Grandma's wailing again brought a big weeping ground.

"Soldiers who sacrificed their lives in the war, US ships which transported us to the south, and Gen Whitcomb who rescued us from supporting the tents and houses..., how can we repay and make it up to them? I have short of years to live, but you young generations should live longer and pay back to them."

Minah and Aunt strongly nodded to Grandma.

국민훈장 무궁화장에 추서된 위트컴 장군

  나진희 선생님이 흥남철수대작전을 자세히 설명했어요. 특히 크리스마스를 사흘 앞둔 날, 남쪽으로 떠난 메러디스 빅토리호 이야기를 들려줄 때 가슴이 뭉클했어요. 민아는 나진희 선생님의 말이 이어질 때 할머니가 또 울까 봐 걱정되었어요.

  1950년 12월 22일 흥남부두에 미군과 한국군 10만 5,000명과 피란민이 몰려 혼잡한 상태였대. 미국 군함과 비행기가 중공군에 폭격을 하는 동안 군함과 상선 약 200척이 흥남철수작전에 동원됐어. 흥남에서 군인들을 배에 태워 남쪽으로 실어 나르기 위한 작전이야. 피란민은 배를 탈 수 없었어. 군인들만 실어나르기도 힘든 상황이었으니까. 흥남부두로 몰려나온 피란민들은 속이 까맣게 탔겠지.
  이 안타까운 장면을 본 현봉학 선생이 용기를 냈어. 10군단장 알몬드 사령관의 민사고문으로 일하는 현봉학 선생이 알몬드 장군에게 피란민도 배를 타게 해달라고 간곡히 부탁했어. 영화 '국제시장'에 보면 "장군, 부탁드립니다. 제발 우리 국민을 도와주세요. 그냥 떠나버리면 피란민들은 중공군에게 몰살당하고 말 겁니다"라고 말하는 장면 그대로였어.

Gen Whitcomb, posthumously honored by Mugunghwa Medal of Order, Civil Merit of Korea

Ms. Na explained us in detail about the Hungnam Evacuation Operation. Especially, the story of the SS Meredith Victory very much impressed us. Minah was nervous that Grandma would cry again.

On 22nd December 1950, there was a big chaos in Hungnam Port, crowded with 105,000 of the US and Korean military troops, and countless war refugees. While US combat aircraft and war ships bombing the Chinese Communist Army, 200 war ships and merchant ships were mobilized for Hungnam Evacuation Operation. Since the ships would be operated for transporting the military troops to south and the space was not enough, the war refugees could not be allowed to board on. The mob of refugees who hastily rushed to Hungnam Port became desperate and dreadfully anxious lest they would lose the chance to board on the ships.

현봉학 선생의 눈물겨운 호소에 알몬드 장군은 군수물자를 버리고 피란민들을 태우라고 명령했어. 그래서 9만 8,000명의 피란민이 남쪽으로 무사히 오게 된 거야. 그때 순이 언니 가족도 온 거지.

가장 많은 인명을 구조한 배로 2004년 기네스북에 등재된 메러디스 빅토리호의 철수 작전은 정말 감동적이야. 흥남부두에서 많은 배가 떠나고 메러디스 빅토리호를 비롯해 몇 척 안 남았을 때였어. 메러디스 빅토리호는 물건을 실어나르는 상선이어서 정원이 60명밖에 안돼. 이미 선원 47명이 타고 있었기 때문에 13명만 더 태울 수 있었어. 아직 배를 타지 못한 피란민들이 울면서 발을 동동 구르고 있었지.

Mr. Hyun, Bonghak, who was then working as an advisor to Gen Almond, the Commanding General of US 10th Corps, watched this tragic scene. He then bravely intervened in that situation imploring Gen Almond for mercy to allow the refugees on board. The Korean drama film Gukjesijang (Ode to my Father in English title) showed the realistic scenes of that day: 'General, please give a big favour for our people. If you leave them on port, they all would be killed by the enemy forces.'

Deeply impressed by Mr. Hyun's pathetic pleading, Gen Almond ordered to throw away all the military supplies from the ship and take the refugees on board. So 98,000 refugees including Sooni's family could safely be on board and evacuated to south.

The story of SS Meredith Victory in Hungnam Evacuation was very impressive. The ship was registered in Guinness Book of world record in 2004 for its world largest humanitarian rescue operation.

Most of the ships anchored in Hungnam port already left to south and only few ships were remained including the SS Meredith Victory. The ship was built to transport trade supplies and goods having only capacity for 60 personnel. 47 crews were already got on board and just the room for 13 personnel were remained available. The war refugees remained in the port cried stamping their feet on the port side.

그때 미 육군 대령들이 승선해서 레너드 라루 선장에게 피란민들을 태워달라고 부탁했어. 아무리 많이 태워도 2,000명 정도의 공간밖에 없었대. 그 순간 레너드 라루 선장이 사람을 살리기로 결단하고 화물칸을 개조했어. 피란민들도 짐을 다 버리고 한 명이라도 더 태우려고 애써서 1만 4,000명이나 탔어.

사흘동안 빽빽하게 타고 남쪽으로 올 때 다섯 명의 아기가 그 배에서 태어났어. 미군이 그 아기들에게 '김치 1, 김치 2, 김치 3, 김치 4, 김치 5'라는 이름을 지어줬대.

나진희 선생님이 말하는 동안 내내 눈물 흘린 할머니가 또 "그 은혜를 어찌 다 갚을고"라고 했어요. 고모가 할머니에게 진정하라며 찬물을 건네면서 말했어요.

"2011년부터 부산지역 신문에 위트컴 장군에 대한 보도가 나오기 시작하면서 추모제와 함께 세미나, 전시회 같은 행사가 열리고 있어요. 부산시민들이 계속 기념하면서 은혜를 갚아 나갈 거예요. 위트컴 장군님의 공이 알려지면서 한묘숙 원장님 장례식도 부산대학교장으로 거행했잖아요."

고모의 말에 할머니와 나진희 선생님은 정말 다행이라고 했어요.

At the moment, some US Army Colonels went on board and proposed Captain Leonard LaRue the rescue of refugees. Since the capacity of the accommodation was only 2,000 personnel at most, Captain LaRue decided to remodel the cargo sections to save the human lives. Therefore, around 14,000 personnel were possible to get on board giving up all of their packings into the sea.

During the three days of voyage to south, five babies were newly born on board in such a congestion circumstances depicted as 'packed like sardines in a can', and the US soldiers named babies, 'Kimchi 1, 2, 3, 3, 4, 5'.

Grandma in tearing all the time during Ms. Na's speaking again said "How can we repay him of his grace?" Aunt handed Grandma cold water to cool her down.

"From 2011, many news of Gen Whitcomb's charities came out, lots of events for him were being held like memorial services, seminars, or exhibits…. Busan citizens would keep memorizing him and tried to repay his grace. As a result, the funeral service of late Ms. Han, Myosook was honorarily sponsored by Busan National University as an honor for the spouse of Gen Whitcomb."

After hearing Aunt, Grandma and Ms. Na spoke in one voice it was fortunate.

"2022년 11월 11일 위트컴 장군님께 국민훈장 중 최고 영예인 무궁화장이 추서되었어요. 전후 대한민국 복구에 전념했던 공을 기려 훈장을 추서한 거죠. 위트컴 장군님이 유엔기념공원에 안장된 지 40년 만이라니 늦었지만 정말 잘된 일이에요."

고모의 말에 할머니가 "최고 훈장받는 게 당연하지"라며 고개를 끄덕였어요.

"부산 지역 초등학생들이 요즘 위트컴 장군님에 대해 배우고 있어요. 위트컴 장군님은 우리나라 전역, 아니 세계적으로 알려야 할 분이에요."

고모의 말에 두 분은 "정말 잘 됐다. 그래야 하고말고"라며 좋아했어요. 어느새 밤 12시가 다 되었고 불을 끄고도 두런두런 얘기가 이어지다가 어느 틈엔가 모두 잠들었어요.

아침에 일어나보니 고모가 누룽지를 끓이고 있었어요. 나진희 선생님과 할머니는 누룽지가 구수하다며 좋아하셨어요. 나진희 선생님은 위트컴 장군님 조형물 제막식 날 다시 오기로 하고 떠났어요.

On 11th Nov 2022, Gen Richard S. Whitcomb was posthumously honored by the Mugunghwa Medal — the most prestigious Order of Civil Merit of Korean Government- for his meritorious performance for reconstruction of post war Korea. The medal was awarded to him 40 years after he was buried in UNMCK, but not too late though it was late.

Grandma nodded and said, "It is rightful for General to be honoured by the highest medal."

"Recently, the elementary school kids in Busan are learning about Gen Whitcomb. Gen Whitcomb should be a model character to be spreaded out to every corner of Korea as well as of the whole world.

Two ladies gladly said "Really really good. It should be like that". Soon, it became midnight. Even though all the light were turned off, the talks still continued, but in a moment everybody was put to sleep.

As I awoke in the morning, Aunt was cooking scorched rice. Grandma and Ms. Na liked scorched rice for its tasty smell. Then Ms. Na left us promising to come again on the day of unveiling ceremony of the statue.

한국인보다 더 한국을 사랑한 위트컴 장군

　방학이 끝나고 서울로 돌아와 2학기를 맞은 민아는 11월 11일을 손꼽아 기다렸어요. '유엔참전용사 국제추모식'에 맞춰 위트컴 장군님 동상 제막식이 열리는 날이거든요.

　드디어 위트컴 장군님 동상 제막식 날이 다가와 교외학습체험 신청을 했어요. 마침 출장을 가게 된 아빠와 함께 부산에 도착하니 할머니가 반갑게 맞아 주었어요. 아빠는 업무를 보고 고모가 안내하기로 했어요.

　청바지 차림의 고모와 달리 할머니와 민아는 핑크색 옷으로 멋을 냈어요. 고모 차를 타고 유엔기념공원 바로 옆에 있는 평화공원을 향해 달렸어요. 벌써 많은 사람이 모여 있었어요. 먼저 와서 기다리던 나진희 선생님의 손을 잡고 할머니가 환하게 웃었어요.

　사람이 많아서 위트컴 장군님 동상을 제대로 볼 수 없었어요. 뒤쪽에서 제막식이 끝나기를 기다렸어요. 이윽고 식이 끝나고 사람들이 빠져나간 뒤에 동상 쪽으로 다가갔어요.

　'한국인보다 더 한국을 사랑한 리차드 위트컴 장군'

　동상 앞 돌판에 새겨진 글씨를 보고 할머니는 "맞아, 딱 맞는 말이야"라고 했어요.

Gen Whitcomb who loved Korea more than Korean people.

Minah returned to Seoul after vacation, and she started second semester. She was looking forward to the day of 11th Nov, the opening ceremony of the statue of Gen Whitcomb.

Finally, the day came, and she applied the off-campus learning experience. Fortunately, her Dad could go with her using his business trip to Busan. Grandma warmly welcomed them again. Dad would do his business and Aunt would guide us.

Grandma and Minah showed off wearing pinky colour while Aunt wore casual jin. Aunt drove to Pyunghwa Park just beside the UNMCK, and many people already there. Ms. Na was also there and Grandma held her hand smiling brightly.

Since too many people gathered, we couldn't see the statue clearly. We waited the closing of the ceremony at backward, and soon after, the ceremony was finished, and we could approach to the statue.

"Gen Whitcomb, the man who loved Korea more than Korean People."

Reading the statement enclosed in the statue, Grandma commented, "Right, just right words."

나지막한 단상 위에 제복 차림의 위트컴 장군님이 서 있었어요. 오른쪽에는 교복을 입은 남학생과 치마저고리를 입은 여자아이, 왼쪽에는 아기를 업은 언니와 고무신을 신은 남자아이 동상도 있었어요. 민아는 치마저고리를 입은 아이가 순이 같기도 하고 진희같기도 해서 눈물이 핑 돌았어요. 할머니와 나진희 선생님은 합창하듯 말했어요.

"어머, 위트컴 장군님 얼굴이랑 똑같아. 어릴 때 봤던 딱 그 모습이야."

Gen Whitcomb was standing in military uniform on the low platform. In his right, there stood statues of a school boy in uniform and a school girl in cotton jacket with skirt. In his left, statue of a girl holding a baby on her back, and a boy wearing rubber shoes. Guessing the girl in cotton clothes seemed Sooni or Jinhee, Minah had full tears on her eyes. Grandma and Ms. Na voiced in chorus "Wow, the statue looks like real figure of Gen Whitcomb. His face looks the same as I ever saw at my young age."

고모가 위트컴 장군님 양쪽에 선 할머니와 나진희 선생님의 사진을 찍었어요. 위트컴 장군님과 한묘숙 원장님의 도움이 없었다면 두 분이 과연 저 자리에 계실까. 그런 생각을 하던 민아의 마음에 잔잔한 감동이 차올랐어요. 민아는 위트컴 장군님 옆에 서서 사진을 찍으며 "땡큐 장군님!"이라고 소리 내서 인사했어요.

동상 뒤편 병풍처럼 펼쳐진 기념비에 위트컴 장군님의 일대기와 업적이 새겨져 있었어요. 기념비 내용을 읽어보고 뒤로 돌아가자 뒷면에 성금을 낸 사람들의 이름이 빼곡하게 담겨 있었어요.

"할머니, 여기 김순이 이름 있어."

"정말? 내 이름이 있어?"

할머니는 돌판에 새겨진 이름을 짚으며 기뻐했어요.

"할머니, 여기 차민아도 있어. 와, 내 이름이다."

고모가 이름에 손가락을 대고 있는 민아의 모습을 찍어주었어요.

11월이어서 조금 쌀쌀했지만 하늘은 구름 한 점 없이 맑고 파랬어요.

"할머니, 저기 하늘 위에서 위트컴 장군님이 다 보고 계실 거야."

민아의 말에 할머니가 고개를 끄덕이며 미소 지었어요.

"그동안 고생도 많이 했지만 고마운 분들 덕분에 여기까지 올 수 있었어. 우리나라가 이만큼 잘 살 게 된 건 다 그분들 덕분이지."

"맞아, 언니, 도움도 받았지만 우리 모두 열심히 살았이. 우리 후손들이 더 열심히 달려 가난한 나라를 많이 도왔으면 좋겠어."

Aunt took pictures of Grandma and Ms. Na standing both side of the statue of General. Minah speculated whether the two ladies could stand there now without the help of Gen Whitcomb and Ms. Han, Myosook, therefore, a deep touching filled her mind. Someone took a picture of Minah standing beside the statue, and Minah loudly spoke out with greeting, "Thank you General!"

On the back side of the statue, the biography and contributions of the Gen Whitcomb was engraved in the commemorative monument. After reading the contents, and turning back, the names of the donators were seen densely occupied.

"Grandma, here is your name, Kim, Sooni" "Oh, really? My name there?"

Grandma was very delighted and touched her name engraved in stone plate.

"Grandma, here is my name, Cha, Minah. Wow, my name too."

Aunt took a picture of Minah who was fingering on her name.

Though the weather was a little bit chilly in Nov, the sky was clear and blue without a single dot of cloud.

"Grandma, Gen Whitcomb may look down all of us from the Heaven above."

Grandma nodded to Minah and smiled.

"Though we had lived hard times in the past, we could reach to current positions with the help of grateful people. We deeply owe our brilliant prosperity to those."

"Right, Sister. We had great help from them, but we also had lived fiercely. I wish our descendents try harder and support the other people of worse countries"

나진희 선생님의 말에 고모가 "요즘 우리나라가 가난한 나라들 많이 돕고 있어요. 원조받다가 원조하는 나라로 탈바꿈한 국가는 대한민국이 유일해요. 잘하고 있으니 걱정마시고, 맛있는 거 먹으러 가요"라고 했어요.

할머니와 나진희 선생님은 매년 위트컴 장군님을 보러 오자며 환하게 웃었어요. 계속 눈물짓던 두 분이 꽃처럼 예쁘게 웃는 모습에 민아는 기분이 날아갈 것 같았어요. 민아는 내년에도 두 할머니와 함께 위트컴 장군님을 뵈러 오기로 마음 먹었어요.

Aunt said to Ms. Na, "Recently, Korea has been providing big support for many poorer countries. 'A nation who was rendered became changed as a nation which can provide the render' is proved Korea only. Our country is now doing well, don't worry. Let's go to have a tasty meal."

Grandma and Ms. Na promised to come here every year to meet Gen Whitcomb and laughed pleasantly. Minah felt like she would be flying away as she saw two old ladies smiling instead of weeping. Minah firmly confirmed in her mind to come to see Gen Whitcomb next year with two Grandmas.

한국인보다 한국을 더 사랑한
위트컴 장군

발행일 1판 1쇄 2024년 8월 31일
지은이 이근미
옮긴이 문영한
그린이 이진주
펴낸이 구충서
디자인 박정미
펴낸곳 도서출판 물망초
출판등록 2014년 10월 21일 제2013-000195호
주소 서울 영등포구 버드나루로 32, 동연빌딩 2층
대표전화 (02)585 9963
전자우편 mulmangcho522@hanmail.net
홈페이지 www.mulmangcho.org
ISBN 979-11-87726-27-2 73810

※ 잘못 만들어진 책은 구입하신 서점에서 바꾸어 드립니다.

General Richard S. Whitcomb loved
Korea more than Koreans

Frist print 31st August 2024
Author Lee, Keun-mi
Translator Moon, Young-han
Artist Lee, Jin-ju
Producer Goo Choong-seo
Book Designer Park Jeong-mi
Publisher Mulmangcho Books
Registered in the Republic of Korea #2013-000195
Floor 2, Dongyeon Building
Beodunaru-ro 32, Yeongdungpo-ku, Seoul,
    South Korea
Telephone +82 (02) 585-9963
E-mail mulmangcho522@hanmail.net
Website www.mulmangcho.org
ISBN 979-11-87726-27-2 73810